FACING DIVORCE IN MICHIGAN?

Useful Information That May Help Your Case

Brent Bowyer, Esq.
Jon M. Midtgard, Esq.

ISBN: 978-1-941645-50-5

Designed and Published by:

Speakeasy Publications
73-03 Bell Blvd #10
Oakland Gardens, NY 11364

www.SpeakeasyMarketingInc.com

888-225-8594

DISCLAIMER

This publication is intended to be informational only. The information in this book is not intended as legal advice. No legal advice is being given, and no attorney-client relationship is intended to be created by reading this material. If you are facing legal issues, whether criminal or civil, seek professional legal counsel to get your questions answered.

American Divorce Association for Men (ADAM)

Metro Detroit – Southfield
2000 Town Center, Suite 2350
Southfield MI 48075

(248) 356-2326

www.AdamDivorceLaw.com

TESTIMONIALS

"I appreciate your advice and work on my case, especially picking it up at such a difficult time in the process. I believe I had one of the more difficult cases, and certainly one of the more uncooperative ex-partners. While I wish my judge were less of a wild card, I was happy to be represented by you. You have been responsive, professional, and from everything I can tell, have given me sound legal advice. Without you and ADAM in my corner, the quality of life for my children would suffer tremendously." ***- Jeff H.***

"All is going well so far with both me and the boys. They are accepting this rather well under the circumstances. I am still involved in their lives with all of their activities. Their mother seems to look rather tired and haggard lately. I think that her new life has really dealt her a bad hand of cards so to speak. Financially, I'm feeling the sting of a scaled down lifestyle, but as long as I can keep my home I'll be grateful.

I hope that all has been well with you. I really enjoyed working with you and every time I hear a commercial on the radio for ADAM, I think about you with a smile on my face and in my heart. I appreciate everything you've done for me and I'll never forget you." ***- James T.***

"I just wanted to send you a note of thanks concerning Brent Bowyer and his staff during my recent divorce. I came to your offices to file for divorce, pretty much ignorant of the whole process. I was assigned to Brent, and in just a few minutes he was able to settle my nerves and lay out the groundwork for what was to come. At the end of the first meeting the complaint was prepared and ready to be filed.

As the legal process kicked in, I was faced with a lot of questions (due mostly to my own ignorance) and decision making. Even when Brent was in court, his legal assistant took my calls. She made sure that Brent addressed all of my questions and concerns promptly and efficiently. After all is said and done, your firm took what I thought would be the most difficult event I had ever been through and made it an almost easy process." ***- Tim G.***

TABLE OF CONTENTS

About The Authors

Attorney Brent Bowyer

Brent Bowyer is a co-owner and partner of the law firm Bowyer and Midtgard, P.C., practicing family law exclusively. Mr. Bowyer earned his B.B.A. from Western Michigan University and his J.D. degree from The John Marshall Law School in Chicago, Ill. He is admitted to the Michigan Supreme Court, Federal District Court, and the U.S. Supreme Court. Mr. Bowyer is a member of the Family Law Section of the State Bar of Michigan, and the Oakland and Wayne County Bar Associations.

Mr. Bowyer has practiced family law exclusively since 1996, litigating hundreds of divorce cases in that time. He has been a repeat guest on the Hardcore Mortgage and Business Show on 97.1 FM talk radio, and has been quoted as an expert in many news media articles including Metro Parent Detroit Magazine. He has also been a guest speaker on the national Fox News Network, and is a frequent speaker at the State Bar of Michigan Family Law Section Mid-Winter Seminars.

Attorney Jon M. Midtgard

Jon M. Midtgard is a co-owner and partner of the law firm Bowyer and Midtgard, P.C. Mr. Midtgard graduated from James Madison College at Michigan State University with honors and the Detroit College of Law; a recipient of a jurisprudence achievement award. Mr. Midtgard is admitted to the State Bar of Michigan and Federal District Court. He has practiced family law exclusively since 1996, and has litigated hundreds of divorce cases in that time.

Jon is a member of the Family Law Section of the State Bar of Michigan, as well as the Oakland County Bar Association for which he has served on the Family Court Committee, American Inns of Court, Law Day Committee, and has participated in Bench/Bar conferences relative to family law. He is also a frequent speaker on family law topics for the Institute of Continuing Legal Education and a member of the Michigan Inter-Professional Association. Jon was a recent guest on the Michigan syndicated news talk radio show, WJIM AM 1240 with Michael Patrick Shiels. He is a repeat guest on the Hardcore Mortgage and Business Show on 97.1 FM, and he was a commentator on 'Due Process' WDIV Channel 4 Detroit.

THINGS TO KNOW BEFORE FILING A DIVORCE IN MICHIGAN

There are many considerations when preparing for a divorce. As a starting point, there are financial matters that should be addressed, and the client should be fully aware of all accounts and balances, all monthly bills and financial obligations, monthly budget, and personal finances.

All too often, we meet with clients who are busy working and hand over their paycheck to their spouse. They don't know what the bills are, what their assets are, or what their debts are. It would be far more beneficial for the client to educate themselves on these financial matters before starting a divorce.

It is also important to get a sense of what assets you have and the value of those assets, whether it's a house, a car, or an investment account. Potential clients should also look at creating a monthly budget when preparing for divorce.

If you have minor children, it's important to take a good look at what type of schedule the children currently have with school and extracurricular activities and how this fits into your work schedule. Discussions will occur during a divorce case regarding custody and parenting time, and you should be prepared to answer questions regarding what a realistic parenting time schedule should be.

It is also a good practice to look at how you are perceived by others. For example, what are you posting on Facebook, Twitter, etc.? What are you telling other people? Divorce is a good time to back away from social media and commenting on anything in your personal life that can be misconstrued and used against you later in the divorce matter.

Prior to a divorce, it's also important to consider how arguments transpire and any potential threats of violence. Are there guns in the house, or are there other things that may be questioned if a divorce is happening and arguing escalates? It's better to position yourself on those issues early before mistakes are made.

What Are Some Valid Reasons For Divorce In Michigan?

There are many possible reasons to seek a divorce. The most common reasons people want to divorce involve adultery or accusations of unfaithfulness. Financial disputes are also very common problems in a marriage.

However, you do not need a reason to file for divorce in Michigan because it is a "no-fault" state. This means you do not have to prove adultery, abuse, abandonment or any other types of issues to have the right to file for a divorce.

In Michigan, if one spouse wants a divorce, it will be granted with no dispute. The disagreements in a divorce case are usually due to all the issues that need to be resolved to complete the divorce. There is no disputing the divorce itself.

People may have disagreements regarding custody, parenting time, financial matters, or division of assets and debts, but they cannot dispute the fact that a divorce itself is requested. There is no way to prevent a divorce if your spouse files for one, at least not through the court system.

Does The State Of Michigan Require A Separation For Filing For Divorce?

Michigan does not require a period of separation for filing for divorce like some other states do. The question then becomes whether or not you continue to live with your spouse at the beginning stages of divorce or throughout the divorce. There is no legal requirement for you to live together during the divorce case.

However, there definitely can be issues with moving out of the house prematurely or moving out without a plan. The preliminary advice is always to stay put and not make plans to move out of the house if there are minor children. Leaving the home is less of a concern when there are no children.

Frequently Asked Questions About Divorce In Michigan

Common Misconceptions People Have About Working With A Divorce Attorney

People have many misconceptions about working with a divorce attorney. If it is the first time they are going through it, they are often unaware of the full process and the scope of work that attorneys do in a divorce.

Some are worried about losing their assets, the children, and they are fearful how much money this will all cost. Our goal as divorce attorneys is to protect the client's assets, negotiate a fair settlement, protect the children's best interests, educate and guide the client through the legal process so they can make informed decisions about their future. First and foremost, however, we want to help the client feel comfortable with the divorce process.

Another misconception is that if the parties are getting along and agree on the issues, they do not need lawyers; they only need to hire a lawyer when there is a dispute. The truth is that even if they think they have an agreement with their spouse on all issues in a divorce, if they own real estate, have investment or retirement accounts, or have minor children, a divorce case can quickly get too complex without legal advice.

The reality is that it is necessary and helpful to have an experienced lawyer to create documents, file and serve the appropriate legal paperwork, navigate the court system and appear on their behalf in court. Without someone knowledgeable educating and guiding an individual through the process, the very problems they fear can easily happen, and it becomes necessary to hire a lawyer to try to fix them.

Other misconceptions are that it's okay for the parties to share an attorney, that it doesn't matter who files first, and that Michigan is not an alimony state. All of these are fallacies.

What Are The Common Reasons For Filing For Divorce?

Potential clients come in with all sorts of reasons as to why they need or want to seek a divorce. A person does not need a reason to file for divorce because Michigan is what's known as a "no-fault state". Nonetheless, there is usually a story to be told, and the client is always asked if there is a reason for filing for divorce. These reasons can sometimes be relevant to the divorce case itself even if it's not necessary to start a divorce case.

Potential clients often will say that they argue with their spouse, cannot get along, or are not on the same page. Some also refer to financial difficulties as a cause for the breakdown of a marriage. Another common reason people cite for wanting a divorce is adultery, either on their part or on the part of their spouse. In other cases, there may be allegations of mental health problems, substance abuse, and even mental or physical abuse.

We help the client work through these reasons and prepare for their divorce. In addition to being a no-fault state, Michigan also does not require divorcing couples to attend any type of couple's therapy prior to getting divorced.

Is There A Typical Divorce Client In Michigan?

Every situation has a unique set of circumstances, but a vast majority of our divorce clients are individuals who are looking for a divorce attorney with expertise in the perspective of men and fathers in divorce, which ADAM specializes in.

We've seen men and women view the divorce process and the issues in a divorce very differently. Men may be more likely to be able to discuss major issues in the divorce case early in the process. At the beginning of a divorce, a man might suggest making a settlement proposal to his wife right away. He will want to open the discussions to determine what to do with the marital home, retirement accounts, savings, cars and debts. A woman, on the other hand, is not usually ready to start discussing those issues so early in the divorce process, even if she's the one who initiated the divorce.

What About Common Law Divorce In Michigan?

Michigan does not recognize common law marriages. Everything starts from the date of marriage forward. So if you are looking at the number of years for something like alimony or division of property, the length of the relationship prior to being married is not relevant in the divorce matter.

Because of this fact, people who are not married and decide to part ways have a very different set of laws and rules that apply to them than would individuals who are married. With no common law marriage, a couple living together and combining their finances without getting married can have unexpected problems when they decide to separate.

WHY IS IT IMPORTANT TO HIRE AN ATTORNEY FOR A DIVORCE CASE?

Should The Couple Hire One Attorney Or Separate Attorneys?

A potential client will often ask if they can hire one lawyer for a divorce matter rather than hiring separate lawyers for each party. This is a common misconception. It is not possible for a husband and wife to share the same divorce attorney. It may be that one of them has an attorney and one of them does not, but this situation is not the same as sharing one attorney.

If the wife hires an attorney, that attorney is giving her legal advice and representing her best interests solely. Her attorney cannot then ethically give the husband legal advice, and must avoid misleading the husband and wife into believing the attorney is representing both parties.

While it is possible to go through a divorce with only one party represented, it is advisable that the party with no attorney at least initially consult with an experienced attorney about their specific circumstances and concerns, and make an educated decision on how to proceed. To rely upon representations made by the spouse's attorney can only lead to confusion and regret regarding decisions made in a divorce matter.

Should Someone Hire An Attorney For Their Divorce Or Represent Themselves?

There's an old saying that the client who represents himself has a fool for a client. This adage holds true all the more today. For a client to represent themselves in a divorce matter, they would need to know the laws in Michigan regarding division of property as well as how custody matters are decided, parenting time, and how child support is calculated if they have minor children.

If there's an issue of spousal support, the do-it-yourself client would also need to know the twelve factors for calculating spousal support and how to determine those issues. When you add the additional requirement that you would need to know how to navigate the court system and how to properly prepare, file and serve paperwork (not just fill out some forms on line), divorce quickly becomes a very overwhelming task to try to handle without a professional.

We frequently meet with potential clients who are considering handling their divorce without an attorney. At a minimum, you should consult with a divorce attorney prior to the divorce case. This will give you a sense of what the issues are in your divorce matter, the pros and cons of hiring an attorney, and then help you to make a more informed decision. There is almost no individual who would be best-served by handling a divorce matter without an attorney.

Another misconception is that you can obtain forms online or go to the courthouse and fill out a few forms and be on your way to completing a divorce. Even under the simplest circumstances, it's important to keep in mind that the employees of the court are prohibited by law from giving legal advice should you need it. It puts them in a very difficult position when someone starts asking questions about how to handle a divorce.

In ADAM's 27 years of divorce practice, we have seen many divorce cases handled very poorly by an individual who had no attorney during the divorce matter. Mistakes are made that quite frankly cannot be fixed later and can affect a client's financial livelihood for the rest of their lives. There's a great deal at stake in a divorce matter when you're dealing with spousal support, real estate, investment accounts, retirement accounts, trusts, or debts. This is without even looking at the issues that can be involved with minor children, such as custody, parenting time, child support, tax exemptions, day care expenses, therapy, private school tuition, and other issues.

Factors That Can Have An Impact On The Granting Of A Divorce

Is It Possible For One Spouse To Prevent The Granting Of A Divorce?

No, it is not possible for one spouse to prevent the granting of a divorce. People may have different reasons for not wanting a divorce such as religious beliefs, or practical considerations like health insurance and other issues. In these situations, it is possible for the parties to agree on a legal separation.

We often hear "I don't want a divorce", or "I should not have to go through this process". Unfortunately, there is no way to prevent the ultimate granting of a divorce if the other spouse files for divorce.

Are There Benefits To Filing For A Divorce First?

Yes, there are benefits to filing first in a divorce situation. A divorce case is a lawsuit and not a joint venture under Michigan state law. The person that files the lawsuit first is the plaintiff. Under Michigan's legal system, there are advantages to being plaintiff as opposed to the defendant.

For example, if there is a hearing or trial, the plaintiff will present their evidence first and would have those types of advantages during any legal proceeding. The plaintiff also has more control from the beginning because they know exactly when the case has been filed, usually before the defendant is aware.

Additionally, Michigan courts allow the plaintiff to request a court order day one in conjunction with the divorce case being filed. The court will sign what is known as an "ex-parte order" (Latin for "without a hearing") which can establish ground rules and make preliminary decisions in the divorce matter and the defendant must comply. Once these decisions are made, they can be difficult to undo later.

For example, if there are minor children, the court can sign an ex-parte order at the beginning that establishes custody, parenting time and child support, including child support amounts. This court order is signed by the judge and entered with the court. The defendant is then bound by this court order even though they had no say in it, and had not presented their side of the story.

The court will also sign what is known as a mutual restraining order against property transfer. These court orders can freeze bank accounts, and take action on other financial accounts and other financial matters.

There are also many other examples of court orders signed at the beginning of a divorce case that can have a major impact and repercussions to the defendant in the case. The plaintiff has control over the substance and the timing of these court orders.

Common Questions Asked In Divorce Cases

What Issues Affect A Divorce Case?

There can be domestic violence issues and/or allegations of physical or mental abuse, real or perceived, in a divorce. These situations can become very complex and adversely affect the circumstances in a divorce case, especially as it pertains to use of the marital home, custody and parenting time.

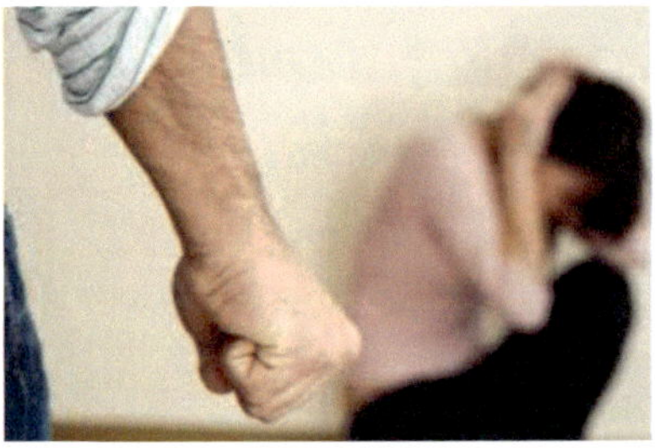

Mistakes can be made when it comes to allegations of abuse that become difficult to undo later. If these circumstances apply to your situation, it is crucial to get advice from an attorney as early as possible.

ADAM not only has expertise in divorce and family law, but also deals directly with criminal charges and child protective services. They know criminal defense matters and can protect you and advise you in any situation.

What Are Some Common Misconceptions People Have About Divorce?

Some common misconceptions of divorce include how long the divorce will take, how much it will cost, the level of difficulty involved with the divorce case, and whether you are required to go to court to get divorced.

It is also a common misbelief that there is no such thing as alimony or spousal support. Another common misconception is defining a divorce as either contested or uncontested when Michigan courts do not differentiate between the two.

Should Someone Choose Mediation vs. The Court Process In A Divorce Case?

Mediation is commonly part of a divorce action. There is no way to independently use mediation and not go to court to become divorced. The only place that a divorce can actually be granted is in a courtroom by a judge so it's not a question of mediation being better than divorce; it's more a question of whether mediation will be necessary during your divorce to resolve issues between the parties. Typically, about 95% of all divorce cases are settled. How those cases settle in the process can vary widely, depending on the clients and the

court system. There are a large majority of cases that end up going through alternative dispute resolution, which can include mediation.

A typical mediation process will involve the divorce clients going to a mediator, normally a third party attorney, and presenting the issues they disagree on. The mediator then makes suggestions and works through the issues with both parties to help reach an agreement. The mediation process is voluntary and, therefore, no one can be forced to use mediation or forced to make an agreement.

The mediation process is a good thing in a divorce matter and is recommended to clients whenever appropriate. The client is always going to be better off with an agreement that they have a say in as opposed to being stuck with a decision from the judge that they have had no say in.

There are ground rules with reaching an agreement on the various issues in a divorce case. First, there can be no enforceable agreement prior to a divorce or legal separation being filed. So, step one is to file for divorce, not coerce your spouse into a written agreement, and then later file for divorce. To reach an agreement prior to filing for divorce runs the risk of any agreement being unenforceable once the case is actually started.

How Is A Successful Outcome In A Divorce Case Defined?

The best way to have a successful outcome is to define, early on, how realistic your expectations are going to be. This is where the experience of your divorce attorney becomes particularly important. It is advisable to cover the specifics with your attorney early on no matter what the issue is, so that you know what is realistic, what is possible, and what is just some nonsense your friend or co-worker told you.

If your friends are telling you there is no way you will have to pay alimony or spousal support to your spouse because they were unfaithful, you should discuss this issue with your attorney and adjust your expectations after they examine your specific situation.

By the way, adultery in and of itself will not necessarily affect a decision to pay spousal support. Also, if you've been told that there is no alimony because you have been married less than ten years, or that Michigan is not an alimony state, both of those statements are untrue.

If you get your preliminary questions answered properly, you will know what to expect, and have a better outcome.

How Long Does It Take To Obtain A Divorce In Michigan?

There are two different timeframes involved with divorce cases in the state of Michigan. There is a 60 day minimum waiting period in divorces where there are no minor children (meaning children over 18 or the parties never had children). There is a six-month minimum waiting period for a divorce where the parties have minor children.

These are minimum waiting periods, not the maximum timeframe. Many factors can affect how long a divorce case will ultimately take from start to finish. Minimizing differences between the parties, working closely with your attorney, providing all required documentation and being available whenever needed all go a long way towards moving the case along and ultimately getting the case settled.

The judge assigned to your case is another important factor and can have an impact on how long your divorce case will ultimately take. It is advantageous to hire an attorney who has expertise in the area of divorce and family law, and experience working with the particular county court system you are dealing with.

Done incorrectly, or in the hands of an inexperienced attorney, a divorce can certainly take much longer. There are many pitfalls along the way that, when not handled properly, can lead to delays and increased costs in a divorce.

Is There Any Way To Fast Track A Divorce Case?

There is no real way to fast track a divorce case, but there is certainly the right way and the wrong way to handle the process and move the case along. The statutory waiting periods are what they are and are generally immutable with some exceptions. It is possible to get a written agreement resolving all issues right away, and be complete in less than the minimum waiting period. This is, however, the exception and not the rule.

To move the matter along smoothly, the client can help by being responsive when their attorney or their spouse's attorney has questions or needs information, be available for meetings and phone calls as needed, appear and being punctual for all scheduled court dates, and keep track of deadlines as they come up on their divorce matter.

The client can also assist by minimizing disputes and not intentionally aggravating their spouse or picking fights over things that, in the big picture, do not matter. A divorce case can be a smooth process, conclude in less time and be less costly when the client remains in contact with their attorney and follows recommendations of their attorney.

The court will allow, for good cause shown, a divorce to be completed short of the statutory waiting periods, 60 days with no children and 180 days with children. However, having any case completed more than a month short of this waiting period is extremely unlikely.

What Determines A Court's Decision On Child Custody?

Michigan law requires that a judge evaluate 12 different factors, which are referred to as the "Best Interests of the Minor Child Factors." "Best interests of the child" means the sum total of the following factors to be considered, evaluated, and determined by the court:

- The love, affection, and other emotional ties existing between the parties involved and the child.

- The capacity and disposition of the parties involved to give the child love, affection, and guidance, and to continue the education and raising of the child in his or her religion or creed, if any.

- The capacity and disposition of the parties involved to provide the child with food, clothing, medical care, or other remedial care recognized and permitted under the laws of this state in place of medical care, and other material needs.

- The length of time the child has lived in a stable, satisfactory environment, and the desirability of maintaining continuity.

- The permanence, as a family unit, of the existing or proposed custodial home or homes.

- The moral fitness of the parties involved.

- The mental and physical health of the parties involved.

- The home, school, and community record of the child.

- The reasonable preference of the child, if the court deems the child to be of sufficient age to express preference.

- The willingness and ability of each of the parties to facilitate and encourage a close and continuing parent-child relationship between the child and other parent, or the child and the parents.

- Domestic violence, regardless of whether the violence was directed against or witnessed by the child.

- Any other factors considered by the court to be relevant to a particular child custody dispute.

While extensive volumes have been written about these individual factors, the overriding consideration is the custody arrangement that will create the least amount of disruption in the child's life.

Central to that discussion is which parent has been the primary caregiver of the child. That is, who does the child look to for his or her daily needs, including health care, schooling, feeding, clothing and nurturing? Men should keep in mind that a custody determination under the law is not necessarily based upon what is "fair" to either parent, per se, but rather what a judge deems to be in the best interests of the child. Further, the factors primarily apply to a parent's capacity to parent.

For instance, a party's mental or physical health will only be relevant to the extent that it has an impact on the parent's ability to care for or set an example for the child. A party's moral fitness will primarily be relevant in terms of that party's ability to set a good moral example for the child.

At What Age Does A Child's Preference Affect The Custody Decision?

The short answer is that there is no magic age. The reasonable preference of the minor child is one of the Best Interest Factors that the judge will consider when determining custody. The key is the term "reasonable."

An extremely young child, typically less than 7 years old, is viewed as too young to express a preference. But the older and more mature the child is, the more likely his or her preference will be considered. That said, the child cannot officially decide where he or she wants to live until the age of 18. That

decision is up to the judge who has jurisdiction over the case.

If a child's preference is to be considered, the court will typically meet with the child privately, and that conversation will technically be confidential. A child will never be asked outright which parent he or she chooses, but rather would be asked different questions that illuminate the judge on their preference.

A client should never bring a child to a court proceeding unless the instructed by the court to do so, regardless of how much the child wants to express their preferences.

Who Gets Child Custody In A Divorce In Michigan?

Do Courts Favor Women When It Comes To Child Custody?

At ADAM, our entire legal team is dedicated to combating gender bias in custody cases. However, it is important to keep in mind that true bias occurs only when the facts are equal and the mother wins solely because she is the mother.

If the mother has been a stay at home parent without any particular parenting deficiencies and the father spends 80 hours a week at work, the mother will have a better chance of winning primary custody under the law. This would not be due to gender bias. However, the reality is that most families today are two income households where both parents are heavily involved in care giving out of necessity.

The concept of joint physical custody, where the children spend more or less equal time with each parent, is becoming much more prevalent. Courts need to be reminded that fathers can and should play an integral part in raising children in spite of their relationship ending with the mother.

What Strategies Are Used To Specifically Support Father's Rights In Child Custody Cases?

Attorneys at ADAM focus on the things their clients do in the care of the children more so than on the deficiencies of the mother. We encourage our clients to document the things they do in everyday life with the kids. We prove to the judge that our client has been integrally involved in the child's upbringing to this point, and that it would not be in the child's best interests to deny that relationship.

We also encourage clients to be well informed and involved in the details of the child's life, including parent-teacher conferences, obtaining report cards, attending doctor and dentist visits, and being involved in extra-curricular activities.

Of course, there are cases where the mother does have issues that the judge should be aware of, and in that situation, we stand ready to prove that placing the child with the mother would be detrimental. In these cases, it is important to refer the matter to appropriate mental health professionals for a psychological evaluation or to utilize a drug or alcohol monitoring expert to provide evidence of concerns in that regard.

What Are The Differences Between Sole Custody And Joint Custody?

In Michigan, a judgment of custody addresses both legal and physical custody. Legal custody is the ability to make decisions on major issues involving the children surrounding their education, health care and religion. Physical custody is where the children primarily reside.

Sole legal custody would provide that parent with exclusive decision-making ability as to where a child goes to school, whether the child gets moved up or held back a grade, whether a child has elective medical procedures or immunizations, and what type of religious education a child may have. A party having sole legal custody also has the ability to change the domicile, or the state where the child is going to live, without the court having to conduct a trial.

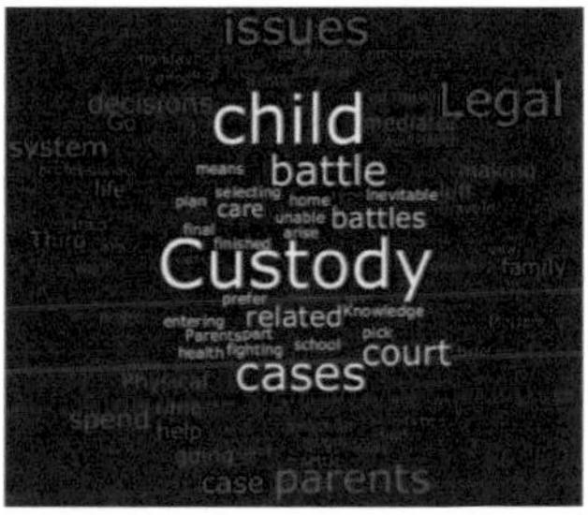

With joint legal custody, both parties are consulted and have a say in all of these decisions. Should one party object to the other parent's decision on an issue, that parent can file a motion with the court, and the judge will determine what is best for the child. As a joint legal custodian, each parent is entitled to school and medical information necessary to participate in this decision-making.

A party that has joint legal custody cannot move more than 100 miles from where he or she lived when the custody action completed without the judge's permission except in limited circumstances. Furthermore, any request to move the child out of the state can be defended by a parent with joint legal custody and would require the court to conduct an evidentiary hearing before making that decision.

Sole physical custody means that the child primarily resides in that parent's household. The other parent would have parenting time. While there is no great statutory definition for the term joint physical custody, in practice it usually means that the children spend enough time in both parents' homes to say that they have two physical residences.

This does not necessarily mean equal parenting time, just that the child spends a substantial amount of time with both parents. Our focus at ADAM has been on parenting time and quality time with the children more than the label of sole or joint physical custody.

How Does ADAM Strategically Help Clients Come To an Amicable Custody Arrangement?

In most cases custody is settled between the parties. While even reasonable minds can disagree on what is in the child's best interest, with a little work on behalf of the attorneys, there can be a meeting of the minds.

At ADAM, our main approach is to encourage settlement between the parties, as a protracted custody and parenting time battle can be expensive and extremely detrimental to the long-term family relationship. We remind our clients that the child's mother will always be the mother, and how the father acts during this process will have a lasting impact.

It is almost always better for the parties to reach an agreement than to have a custody and parenting time arrangement imposed upon the parents. Where parties cannot agree on an arrangement it is best to accentuate the positive as to the client's parenting rather than go on the attack and look to destroy the other parent.

Courts are much more impressed with what our client brings to the table in terms of providing a good environment for the child than they are with vicious attacks on the other side. To the extent negative facts about the mother must be presented, there is no choice but to do so. However, keeping it positive and focused on the child is always the better path whenever possible.

Joint Physical Custody And Supervised Visitation Rights

Who Works Out The Specific Schedule And Details For Joint Physical Custody? Does The Court Have to Officially Approve Of The Arrangements, Along With Any Changes Throughout The Years?

Ideally, the parents can decide a specific schedule for parenting time, as one would hope they know what's best for their own child. But when the parents cannot agree, it is common for negotiation to take place between their respective attorneys. If the parties cannot agree with the help of their attorneys, then they can try to resolve their matter with the help of the Friend of the Court or a private mediator.

Many counties have policies or guidelines for various parenting time schedules but it is important to know that those guidelines are not the final say, and that ultimately only the judge can establish a custody and parenting time arrangement if the parties disagree.

Typically, the judge will approve a clearly written custody and parenting time agreement reached by the parents and sign an order or judgment containing the same provisions.

Some judges will inspect the custody and parenting time provisions more closely than others. It helps to have an experienced attorney who knows each judges' policies and preferences so that you can be prepared to get the orders approved.

The same thing applies to orders modifying custody or parenting time down the road. Some judges would accept a consent order and sign off on it without a hearing while others will require the parties to appear in order to ensure that the order is in the best interests of the child.

Under What Circumstances Will The Court Order 'Supervised Visitation Rights'? How Do They Work?

Supervised parenting time is ordered in very few cases. However, it can happen when there is some question as to the child's safety or welfare while in one of the parent's care. This could be when domestic violence has been alleged or proven, when child abuse has been an issue, or when the parent has a criminal, substance abuse, or mental health history.

Supervised parenting time will also be ordered if, for whatever reason, the child has been separated from the parent for a lengthy period of time and they need to get reacquainted. In limited cases, the supervision could be done by the other parent or another family member.

Sometimes, a court will ask a mutual acquaintance or family member known to the child to be present during the parenting time. When this is not possible, the court may order supervised parenting time through a counseling center or other facility that specializes in supervising visits.

ADAM has always encouraged clients to work with the supervised plan as scheduled and continue to take the steps necessary to move away from that limited parenting time into a regular custody and parenting time arrangement. Conversely, we advocate supervised parenting time for mothers with these types of issues to continue until she can prove that the child is safe and well cared for with her unsupervised.

How Do Courts Handle Visitation Rights for Other Family Members (grandparents, stepparents, etc.)?

Normally, extended family members or stepparents have visitation when their relative has time with the child. Under Michigan statute, a grandparent has a right to petition the court for

parenting time with the child if that grandparent's child is unavailable to exercise the parenting time, for example, if they are deceased, incarcerated, or stationed overseas with the military.

The grandparent would have to establish a longstanding relationship with the grandchild and prove that a disruption in their parenting time with the child would be detrimental to that child's health and well being.

CHILD SUPPORT AND HOW DOES IT WORK

When Is Child Support Required?

Child support must be addressed in every custody or parenting time order. Child support is governed by the Michigan Child Support Formula, which is a numerical formula written directly into the statute. The formula takes into account both parties' incomes, minus certain deductions, the percentage of overnight parenting time each party has and an allocation of child-care and health care premium expenses.

There is no child support while the parties are still living together, as they would maintain the financial status quo as to payment of expenses in a manner similar to prior to the matter being filed.

Judges are required to order child support pursuant to the Michigan Child Support Formula at the conclusion of any case for divorce, custody, paternity or separate maintenance (legal separation). If the parties wish to deviate from the formula, they must first inform the judge what the support amount would have been pursuant to the formula and indicate why it would be in the child's best interest to deviate from this amount.

A deviation from the formula could be due to a separate arrangement to share expenses for the child, such as travel expenses if the parties live far apart, special needs of the child or other property settlement considerations between the parties. The judge would make a finding either in court or in the Judgment that this is acceptable.

Parties should keep in mind that child support is always modifiable upon a change of circumstances, which means if they give something up in order to avoid child support, the other parent could seek to have it ordered down the road. In certain cases where the child or parent is receiving public assistance, the court cannot deviate from the child support formula and child support must be paid through the Friend of the Court via income withholding order.

When Is The Best Time For A Parent To File For Child Support?

Child support can be requested in any case involving minor children at the outset of the proceedings. Normally, child support is paid when the parties live in separate residences. If the parents are separated at the time, child support can be ordered retroactive to when that case is filed.

What Determines The Payment Amount For Child Support?

Child support is governed by the Michigan Child Support Formula, which is a numerical formula written directly into the statute. The formula takes into account both parties' incomes minus certain deductions, the percentage of overnight parenting time each party has and an allocation of child care and health care premium expenses.

How Long Is A Parent Legally Required To Pay Child Support? Are There Extenuating Circumstances That Would Require A Parent To Pay Child Support For A Longer Period Of Time?

Child support is payable until the child turns 18 or graduates from high school, whichever comes first. If a child has not graduated from high school when he or she turns 18, child support may continue until graduation but not beyond age 19 years, 6 months. In order for child support to continue after the child turns 18, the child must live with the payee parent full time, or attend a residential high school and be taking enough classes to graduate by age 19 ½.

The parties may agree to continue support beyond age 18 and graduation from high school, but there are no provisions for support to be ordered by a court. Parties often put provisions for college education expenses in their judgments of divorce which are enforceable.

If a parent is caring for an adult child with special needs, that circumstance could be relevant in that party seeking spousal support from the other parent.

What Happens If A Parent Is Not Able To Make Child Support Payments?

What Should Someone Do If Their Ex-wife Refuses To Make Required Child Support Payments?

Child support is enforceable by a number of methods. The Friend of the Court is set up to keep accounting and take enforcement action against payers of support. A payee should contact the Friend of the Court and seek enforcement against the other parent who is refusing or otherwise failing to pay.

What Happens When She Falls Behind On Child Support Payments?

The Friend of the Court will seek an Order to Show Cause which would be served on the non-paying parent. That parent would be required to appear before the court and explain why she should not be held in contempt of court, and what enforcement mechanisms are necessary to get her caught up in support.

Should the non-paying parent fail to appear at the Show Cause hearing, a bench warrant would typically be ordered for their arrest. Chronic failure to pay child support in cases where the Court deems the payer able to pay may lead to charges by the county prosecutor of felony non-support under Michigan's criminal code.

The Friend of the Court is often very busy and backed up in these support actions, and it is usually much quicker to hire your own attorney to enforce the support order. Your attorney would obtain an order for the payer to show cause and have her personally served.

The father's attorney would seek sanctions and attorney fees against the mother for failure to pay. Sanctions could include the suspension of the mother's driver's license, occupational license, or passport, as well as reporting to a credit agency, garnishment of bank accounts, placing a lien on the payer's home, among other enforcement options.

Under What Circumstances Can A Temporary Or Permanent Modification Be Made To Child Support Payments?

Child support is always subject to modification on the basis of a change of circumstances. The parties are entitled to regular review of the current order by the Friend of the Court every 3 years, but can always file a motion with the court to increase or decrease support and related expenses if there has been a change of circumstances. This could include a loss of employment, layoff, injury or illness, change of jobs, retirement, or many other factors.

It is important to note that child support is typically not subject to retroactive modification, which means the court will not order a decrease or an increase back to when circumstances changed, but rather will only go back to when the motion is filed and served upon the other party. Therefore, it is important to file a motion as soon as possible after the change of circumstances has occurred in order to avoid being subject to an inaccurate support amount in the interim.

It is common in cases of layoff that support would be modified based upon unemployment benefits with a requirement that the person paying support report to the Friend of the Court when she gets back to work so that support can be re-adjusted.

What Sets Your Firm Apart in Handling Divorce Matters for Men?

As a firm, ADAM has been litigating family law matters for men for over 27 years. We have nagivated thousands of men through this difficult process over that time. Along the way, we have been zealous advocates for husbands and fathers with the legal experience to back up our positions.

The attorneys at ADAM have chosen to be divorce and custody lawyers for men, as opposed to so many other lawyers who see family law as something they have to do to make ends meet.

We are heavily involved in legal association groups dealing in divorce and custody, and we are regularly asked to participate in seminars to educate other lawyers. ADAM attorneys are known in the legal community (judges, Friend of the Court personnel, mediators) as credible, conscientious and skilled lawyers.

The fact is, when you focus on one area of law, family law, and further specialize in representing the unique interests of husbands and fathers in family law, you do it better.

Made in the USA
Monee, IL
05 November 2026

67385069R00031